Crafts for
Thanksgiving

Crafts for THANKSGIVING

by Kathy Ross

Illustrated by Sharon Lane Holm

Holiday Crafts for Kids
The Millbrook Press
Brookfield, Connecticut

I am
thankful
for

my mom
and dad!

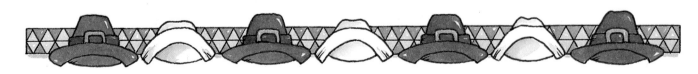

For Greyson and Allison—K.R.
For Michael—S.L.H.

Library of Congress Cataloging-in-Publication Data
Ross, Kathy (Katharine Reynolds), 1948–
Crafts for Thanksgiving / by Kathy Ross:
illustrated by Sharon Lane Holm
p. cm.— (Holiday crafts for kids)
ISBN 1-56294-535-1 (lib.bdg.) ISBN 1-56294-682-X (pbk.)
Summary: Presents twenty simple craft projects that
young children can make from everyday materials.
1. Thanksgiving decorations—Juvenile literature. 2. Handicraft—
Juvenile literature. [1. Thanksgiving decorations. 2. Handicraft.]
I. Holm, Sharon Lane, ill. II. Title. III. Series.
TT900.T5R67 1995 745.594'1—dc20 94-48301 CIP AC

Published by The Millbrook Press
2 Old New Milford Road
Brookfield, Connecticut 06804

Contents

Happy Thanksgiving!

Thanksgiving is celebrated in the United States on the third Thursday of November and in Canada on the second Monday in October. It is a time when friends and family like to celebrate and give thanks for the blessings of the year.

In New England the first traditional Thanksgiving was celebrated by the Plymouth colonists. These early settlers, called Pilgrims, had come to America in the 1600s to escape religious persecution. Their first winter in their new home had been very hard. Native Americans showed the Pilgrims how to grow the corn they needed to survive the difficult winters. Together the Pilgrims and the Native Americans celebrated and gave thanks for a good harvest. This harvest festival began the Thanksgiving Day tradition.

Today Thanksgiving is celebrated by families and friends enjoying a big Thanksgiving meal. The Thanksgiving meal usually includes roast turkey with lots of delicious side dishes. Many families set aside some time to give thanks just as the Pilgrims and Native Americans did so many years ago.

Mayflower Wall Hanging

The Pilgrims made the long journey from England to America on a ship called the *Mayflower*.

Here is what you need:

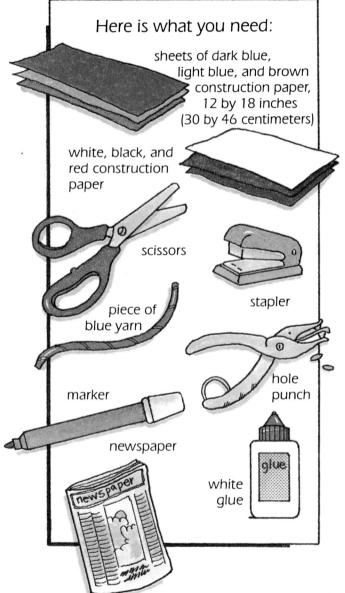

sheets of dark blue, light blue, and brown construction paper, 12 by 18 inches (30 by 46 centimeters)

white, black, and red construction paper

scissors

stapler

piece of blue yarn

hole punch

marker

newspaper

white glue

Here is what you do:

1. Cut waves along one side of the dark blue paper. Fold the waves about one third of the way up to form a pocket and staple the sides to hold the pocket in place. This will be the water. Staple the light blue paper behind the top of the water for the sky.

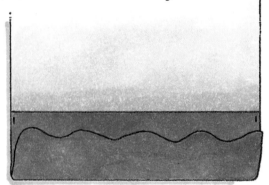

2. Fold the brown sheet of paper in half and cut out

two identical boat shapes. Write "Mayflower" across the side. Staple around the sides and bottom of the ship and stuff some crumpled newspaper inside to puff it out. Put the ship in the wave pocket and glue it in place.

 Cut three masts from black paper and three sails from white paper and glue them in place. Cut red triangle flags and glue them to the top of each mast.

4. Punch a hole in each side at the top of the picture, and tie yarn through the holes.

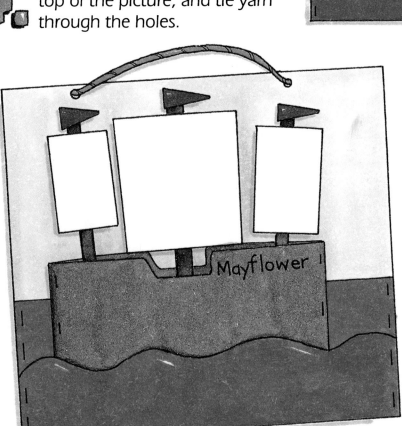

Find a wall for your ship to sail across.

Sailing Ship Puppet

The Pilgrims landed at Plymouth Rock.

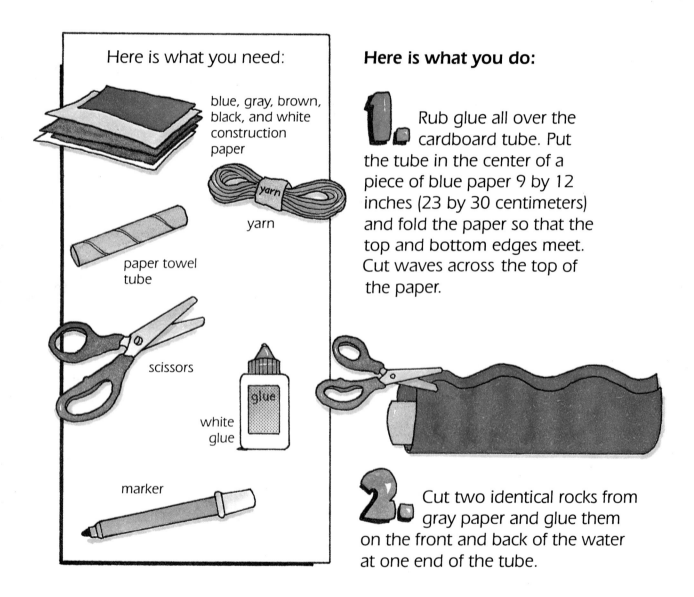

Here is what you need:

blue, gray, brown, black, and white construction paper

yarn

paper towel tube

scissors

white glue

marker

Here is what you do:

1. Rub glue all over the cardboard tube. Put the tube in the center of a piece of blue paper 9 by 12 inches (23 by 30 centimeters) and fold the paper so that the top and bottom edges meet. Cut waves across the top of the paper.

2. Cut two identical rocks from gray paper and glue them on the front and back of the water at one end of the tube.

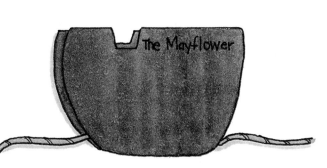

3. Fold a sheet of brown paper and cut out a ship, with the bottom of the ship on the fold so that the ship has two sides. Insert a 3-foot-long (1 meter) piece of yarn in the fold of the ship leaving an equal length sticking out of each side. Glue the ship's sides together.

4. Cut two masts from black paper and stick their bottom sections in between the top of the glued ship while the glue is still wet. Glue sails cut from white paper to the masts. Write "Mayflower" on both sides of the ship and "Plymouth Rock" on both sides of the rock.

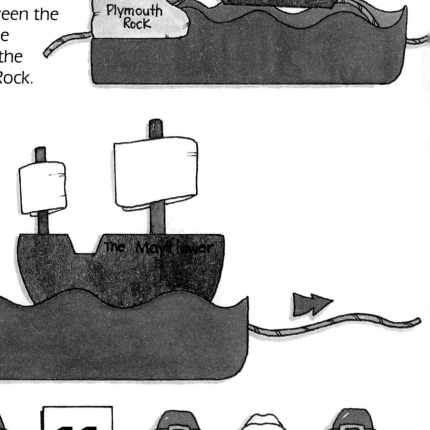

5. Slip the ship in between the paper waves. Pull the string back and forth to sail the ship to and from Plymouth Rock.

Thankful Hands
Pilgrim Boy

The Pilgrims were thankful for many things on the first Thanksgiving. Make a Pilgrim person that looks like you and write on the hands what you are thankful for this Thanksgiving.

Here is what you need:

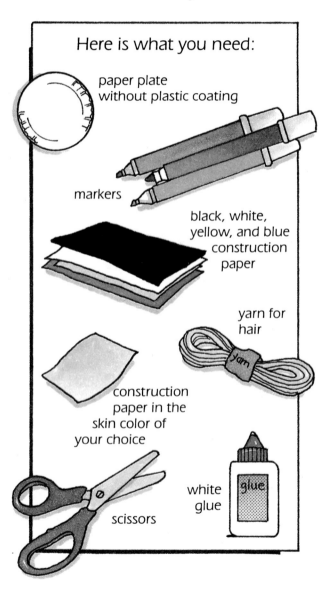

paper plate without plastic coating

markers

black, white, yellow, and blue construction paper

yarn for hair

construction paper in the skin color of your choice

scissors

white glue

Here is what you do:

1. If the paper plate is not close to your skin color, use markers to color it. Draw on a face with markers. Cut bits of yarn and glue them on for hair.

2. Cut a Pilgrim hat from black paper and glue it to the head. Cut a band for the hat from blue paper and a buckle from yellow paper and glue them in place.

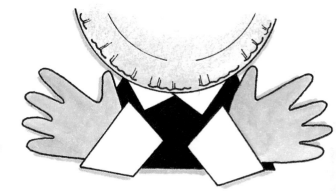

3. Cut a triangle-shaped piece from black paper and glue the point behind the head so that the bottom forms shoulders.

4. Trace your hands onto the skin-colored construction paper and cut them out. Glue them on each side of the Pilgrim as though they were being held "palms up" in front of him.

Cut cuffs and a collar from white paper and glue them in place.

5. On the right hand write "On this Thanksgiving I am thankful . . .," and on the left hand write what you are thankful for and the date.

On this Thanksgiving I am thankful

for my dog Randy.

Hang up your pilgrim so everyone will know what you are thankful for on Thanksgiving.

Thankful Hands
Pilgrim Girl

Here is what you need:

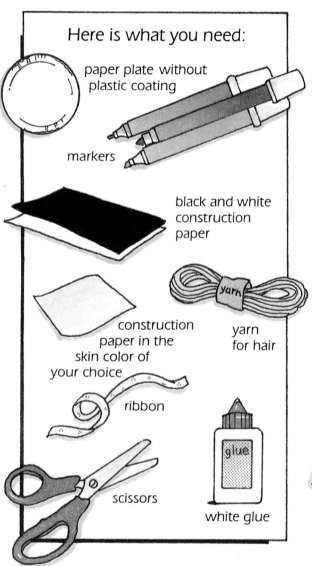

paper plate without plastic coating

markers

black and white construction paper

construction paper in the skin color of your choice

yarn for hair

ribbon

scissors

white glue

Here is what you do:

1. If the plate is not close to your skin color, use markers to color it. Draw on a face with markers. Cut bits of yarn and glue them on for hair.

2. Cut three long rectangles from white paper and glue them across the top and sides of the head to make a hat.

While the glue is still wet, fold the bottom corners of the hat up and glue a piece of ribbon under each side of the hat. Tie the ends of the ribbon in a bow at the bottom of the face. Glue the bow to the plate.

3. Cut a triangle-shaped piece from black paper, and glue the point behind the head so that the bottom forms shoulders.

4. Trace your hands onto skin-colored construction paper and cut them out. Glue them on each side of the Pilgrim as though they were being held "palms up" in front of her. Cut cuffs and collar from white paper and glue them in place.

5. On the right hand write "On this Thanksgiving I am thankful for . . .," and on the left hand write what you are thankful for and the date.

You might want to make a boy Pilgrim and a girl Pilgrim and hang them up together.

Headband Napkin Rings

Native Americans shared the first Thanksgiving with the Pilgrims.
Make these napkin rings to use at your Thanksgiving celebration.

Here is what you need:

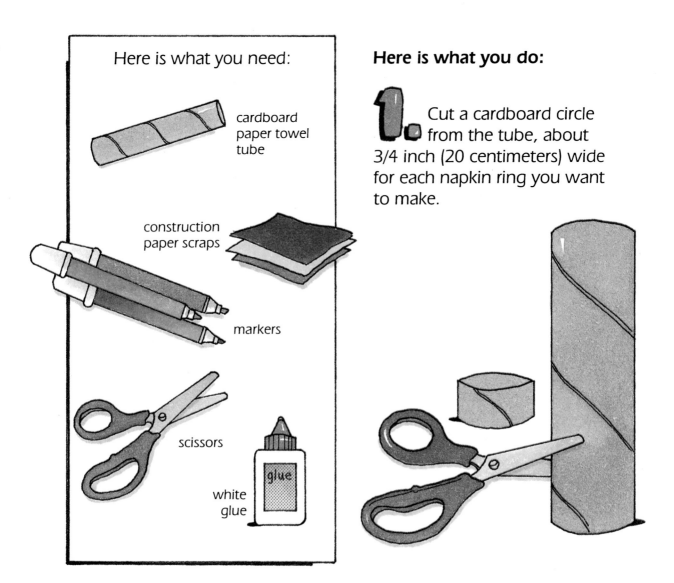

cardboard
paper towel
tube

construction
paper scraps

markers

scissors

white
glue

Here is what you do:

1. Cut a cardboard circle from the tube, about 3/4 inch (20 centimeters) wide for each napkin ring you want to make.

2. Use markers to draw a Native American design on the tube.

3. Cut a tiny feather from construction paper. Fringe both sides to make it look more featherlike. Glue the base of the feather inside the band.

Make lots of napkin rings using different designs and colors.

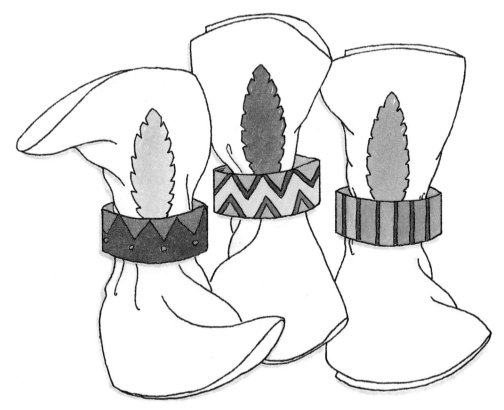

Cornucopia Door Hanging

The cornucopia, or horn of plenty, is a Thanksgiving symbol of the abundance of food from the fall harvest.

Here is what you need:

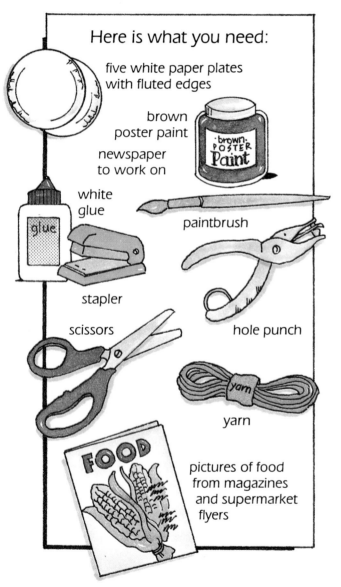

five white paper plates with fluted edges

brown poster paint

newspaper to work on

white glue

paintbrush

stapler

scissors

hole punch

yarn

pictures of food from magazines and supermarket flyers

Here is what you do:

1. Overlap and staple four paper plates together in a row so that the fluted edge of each one is showing on the right. Cut the plates into a horn shape that curves on the end.

2. Cut the center out of a paper plate and staple the rim to the left side of the cornucopia to form the opening. Paint the cornucopia brown and let it dry.

3. Cut out pictures of fruits and vegetables from magazines and supermarket flyers. Fill the opening of the cornucopia with the pictures. Glue the pictures in place.

4. To hang your cornucopia, punch two holes at the top and run a piece of yarn through them. Knot the ends together.

This cornucopia would look wonderful on your front door this Thanksgiving.

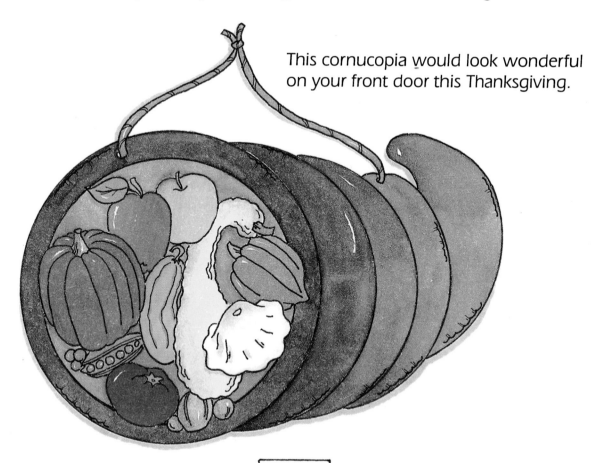

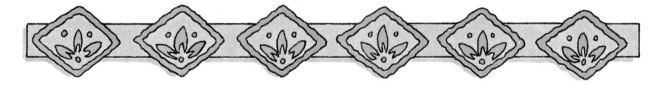

Indian Corn Kernel Magnets

Native Americans showed the Pilgrims how to grow corn.

Here is what you need:

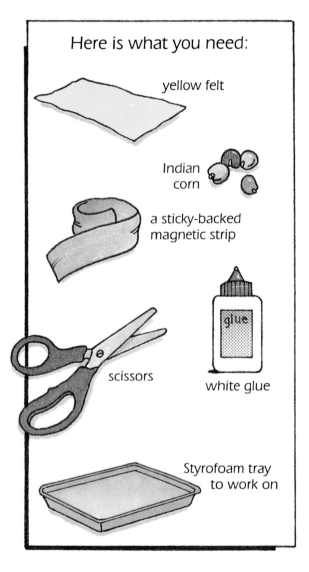

yellow felt

Indian corn

a sticky-backed magnetic strip

scissors

white glue

Styrofoam tray to work on

Here is what you do:

1. Remove several kernels of corn from the cob. Arrange six or seven kernels of a similar color into a flower-shaped circle. Put the points of the kernels toward the center. Choose a kernel of a different color for the center of the flower.

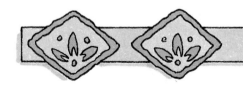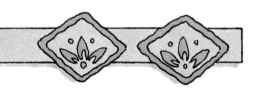

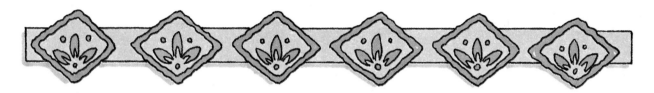

2. Cut a circle of yellow felt the same size as the corn-kernel flower. Cover the circle with white glue and arrange the flower on the felt circle. Put the flower on the Styrofoam tray and cover it completely with white glue. Some glue may run onto the tray. This extra glue can be broken off when it is dry.

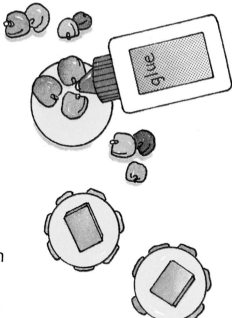

3. When the flower is completely dry, peel it off the Styrofoam tray and break off the extra glue. Press a piece of magnetic strip on its back. You can stick the flower on your refrigerator or on anything else made of metal.

Happy
Thanksgiving
Mom!
mike

need:
Turkey, stuffing
cranberries
potatoes
yams

A set of these flower magnets in different shades would make a very nice Thanksgiving surprise.

Set the Table Poster

Do you know how to set the table for your Thanksgiving feast?

Here is what you need:

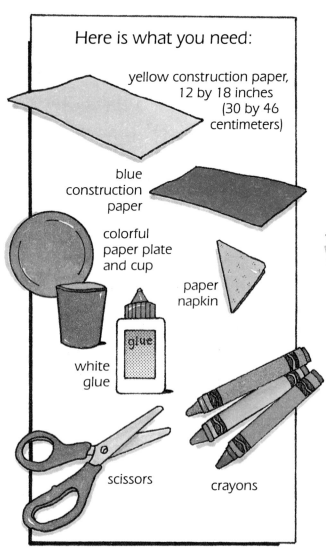

yellow construction paper, 12 by 18 inches (30 by 46 centimeters)

blue construction paper

colorful paper plate and cup

paper napkin

white glue

scissors

crayons

Here is what you do:

1. The large sheet of yellow paper will be the place mat. Decorate it with crayons and write your name at the top.

2. Glue the paper plate to the middle of the mat and the cup to the top right-hand corner. If your plate and cup are plain, you can decorate them with crayons.

3. Cut knife, fork, and spoon shapes from blue paper. Use real silverware as patterns for tracing.

4. Fold a paper napkin and glue it shut. Glue the napkin to the mat on the left side of the plate. Glue the fork on top of the napkin and the knife and spoon onto the mat on the other side of the plate.

Even if you don't need a reminder of how to set the table, this project makes a great poster.

Kathy's Place

Pumpkin Centerpiece

Make a centerpiece for your Thanksgiving table.

Here is what you need:

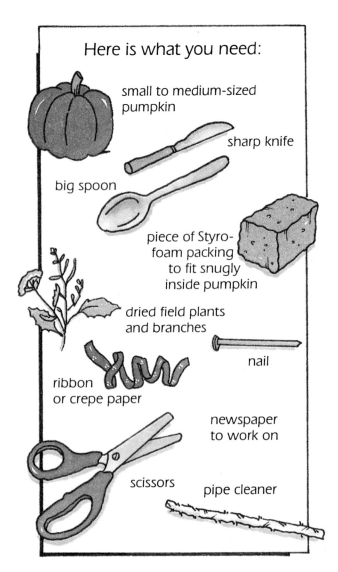

small to medium-sized pumpkin

sharp knife

big spoon

piece of Styro-foam packing to fit snugly inside pumpkin

dried field plants and branches

nail

ribbon or crepe paper

newspaper to work on

scissors

pipe cleaner

Here is what you do:

1. Ask a grownup to cut the top off the pumpkin. Clean the loose seeds and pulp out of the inside.

2. Break off a piece of Styro-foam packing that will fit tightly in the bottom of your pumpkin. Using the nail, poke a hole in the Styrofoam for each plant and branch you are going to put in the pumpkin.

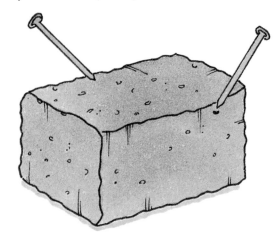

 Wedge the Styrofoam into the bottom of the pumpkin. Fill the pumpkin with dried plants and branches by pushing their stems into the holes in the Styrofoam.

4. Tie several loops of ribbon or crepe paper around one end of a pipe cleaner. Fold the top of the pipe cleaner over the ribbon to hold it in place. Poke the other end into the Styrofoam so that the ribbon is sticking out of the top of the pumpkin.

If you set this pumpkin centerpiece on a table, be sure to put the pumpkin on top of a small plate.

Felt Hot Pad

This hot pad would be very useful at any Thanksgiving feast.

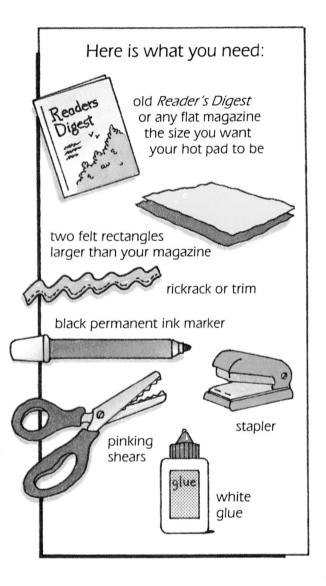

Here is what you need:

old *Reader's Digest* or any flat magazine the size you want your hot pad to be

two felt rectangles larger than your magazine

rickrack or trim

black permanent ink marker

pinking shears

stapler

glue

white glue

Here is what you do:

1. Place a *Reader's Digest* magazine between two felt rectangles and staple them together on all four sides as close to the magazine as possible. Trim the extra felt from around the staples. Pinking shears make a nice edge.

2. Glue trim or rickrack over the staples to cover them.

3. Using a black permanent ink marker, draw or trace a leaf shape on the top side of the hot pad.

Put this hot pad under something delicious on your Thanksgiving table.

Boy Pilgrim Hat Favor

Make Pilgrim hat favors for everyone at your Thanksgiving table.

Here is what you need:

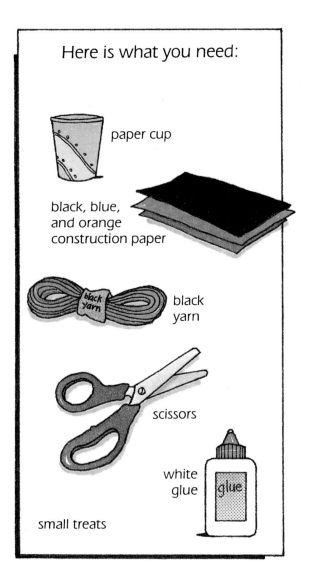

paper cup

black, blue, and orange construction paper

black yarn

scissors

white glue

small treats

Here is what you do:

1. Cut the bottom out of a paper cup. Cover the outside of the cup with glue and wrap the cup in black yarn until it is completely covered.

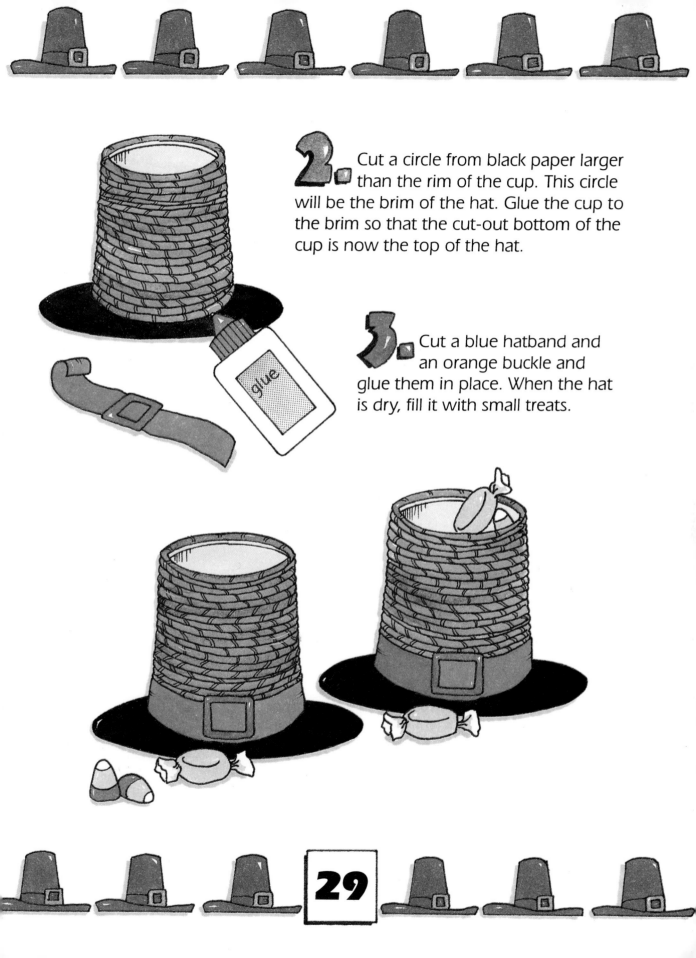

2. Cut a circle from black paper larger than the rim of the cup. This circle will be the brim of the hat. Glue the cup to the brim so that the cut-out bottom of the cup is now the top of the hat.

3. Cut a blue hatband and an orange buckle and glue them in place. When the hat is dry, fill it with small treats.

Girl Pilgrim Hat Favor

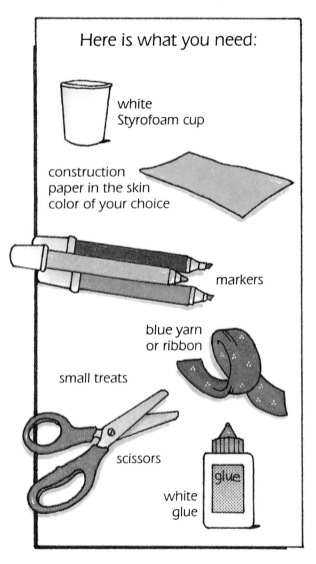

Here is what you need:

white
Styrofoam cup

construction
paper in the skin
color of your choice

markers

blue yarn
or ribbon

small treats

scissors

white
glue

Here is what you do:

1. Cut a circle from construction paper slightly larger than the opening of the cup. Draw a face in the middle of the circle and then draw hair around the face.

2. Fill the cup with treats wrapped in plastic wrap. Rub glue around the inside edge of the cup. Place the face over the opening of the cup and tuck the edges down around the treats.

3. Glue a yarn bow at the chin of the face. When the glue has dried, set the favor on its side.

Soft Sculpture Turkey

The traditional bird of Thanksgiving is the turkey. Make this little turkey to decorate a corner of your home.

Here is what you need:

craft feathers

old knit glove

two eyes that wiggle

scraps of red and orange felt

cotton balls

scissors

white glue

Here is what you do:

1. Stuff the glove with cotton balls. Turn the edges inside and glue them together. You may need to hold the edges shut until they are dry. You can do this with a large paper clip or a clamping clothespin.

2. Poke lots of pretty craft feathers between and around the fingers of the glove. Cut a beak from orange felt and a wattle, the turkey's red throat, from red felt and glue them on the side of the thumb. Glue on two wiggle eyes to complete your bird.

Turkey Wreath

This turkey is to hang on your front door.

Here is what you need:

paper plate without plastic coating

brown poster paint

paintbrush

red, orange, blue, green, yellow, and brown construction paper

scissors

white glue

pencil

hole punch

yarn

newspaper to work on

Here is what you do:

1. Cut the center out of a paper plate so that the rim forms a wreath. Paint the rim brown and let it dry. Punch a hole in the plate and tie a loop of yarn through for a hanger.

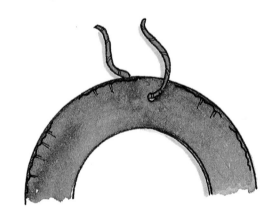

2. Cut a head for the turkey from brown paper and glue it to the bottom front

of the wreath. Cut eyes, a beak, and a wattle from paper and glue them in place on the head. Cut legs from orange paper and glue them so that they hang below the head.

5. To make feathers for the turkey, cut lots of 4-inch (10-centimeter) strips from different colors of paper. Wrap each strip tightly around a pencil and carefully slide the pencil out of the rolled paper. Fill the entire wreath with paper curls.

Gobble, gobble!

Hands and Feet Turkey

Surprise someone this Thanksgiving with a turkey
made from your own hands and feet.

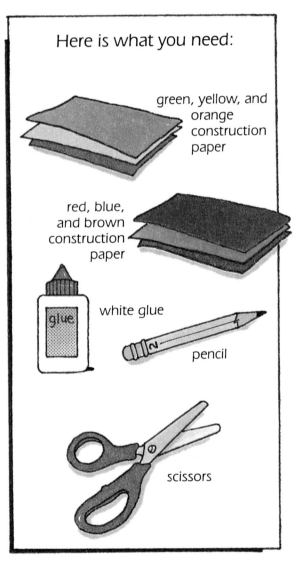

Here is what you need:

green, yellow, and orange construction paper

red, blue, and brown construction paper

white glue

pencil

scissors

Here is what you do:

1. On brown paper, trace both your feet. Cut the paper feet out. Glue the feet together at the heel, so that the feet fan out at the toes. This will be the body of the turkey.

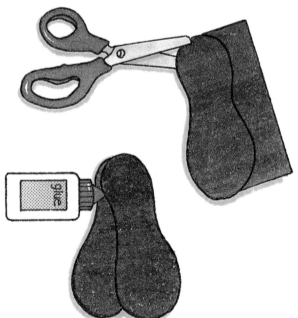

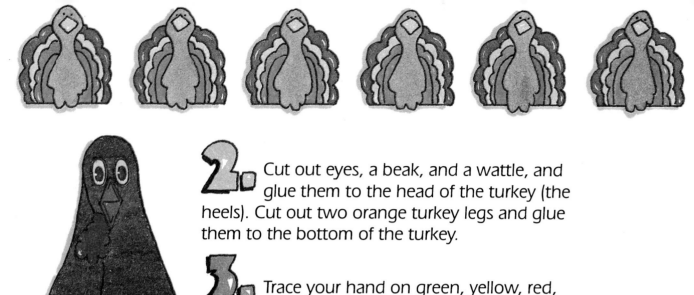

2. Cut out eyes, a beak, and a wattle, and glue them to the head of the turkey (the heels). Cut out two orange turkey legs and glue them to the bottom of the turkey.

3. Trace your hand on green, yellow, red, blue, and orange paper. Cut out three orange hands and one hand from each of the other colors. Glue one orange hand on each side of the turkey for wings. Fan out the other five hands and glue them behind the turkey to form the tail.

Write the date on the back of the turkey so you can see how much your hands and feet will have grown by next Thanksgiving.

37

Magazine House

On Thanksgiving we are thankful for our homes.

Here is what you need:

piece of construction paper, 12 by 18 inches (30 by 46 centimeters)

brown and black construction paper

old home-decorating magazine

white glue

scissors

marker

Here is what you do:

1. To form a house, fold the two sides of the large sheet of paper to meet at the middle, so that each side opens and shuts. Cut a triangle-shaped roof for the house from brown paper and glue it to the top of the flaps of the closed house. Cut from the bottom of the triangle to the point so that the roof and house will open and shut together. Cut a chimney from black paper and glue it on the roof.

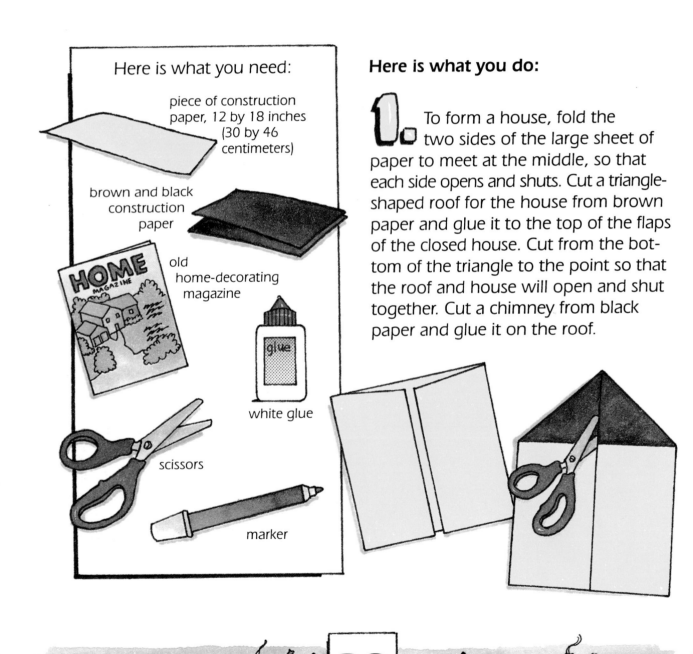

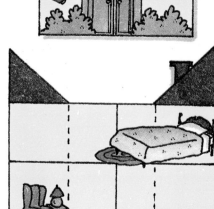

2. Look through old magazines to find a door and windows for the house. You might also want to add a fence and shrubbery. Glue the details in place.

3. Open the house and divide the inside into four rooms, using a marker. Look through old magazines to find furnishings for all the rooms in your house. Don't forget such details as rugs, pictures, and plants. Arrange the furnishings and glue them in place.

You can use the same idea to make an apartment house, a store, a fire station, or any other building you'd like to make.

House Napkin Holder

Here is what you need:

medium-sized food box

two identical envelopes wider than the food box

construction paper in different colors

scissors

white glue

markers

Here is what you do:

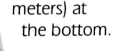

1. Open the flap of one envelope so that it looks like a house. If the envelopes are white, you might want to color them with markers. Place one envelope so that it overlaps the food box slightly on each side. Trace around the pointed flap of the envelope and follow the lines to cut away the portion of the box above the envelope flap. Do the same thing on the other side of the box. Cut away both sides of the box leaving only about 1/4 inch (6 millimeters) at the bottom.

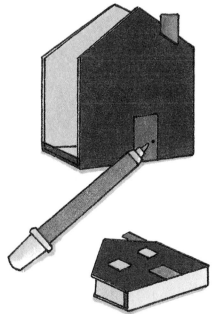

2. Glue an envelope to each side of the box. Cut paper to fit inside the napkin holder to line it and glue the paper in place.

3. Cut doors, windows, and chimneys from construction paper and draw details with markers. Glue these to both sides of the house.

4. Let this project dry with one side of the house facedown.

Fill the house with napkins and surprise someone with this useful gift.

Thanksgiving Plate Collage

On Thanksgiving we give thanks for our food.

Here is what you need:

brown, green, and orange construction paper

dinner-sized uncoated paper plate

fiberfill

brown and yellow poster paint

scissors

paintbrush

white glue

hole punch

newspaper to work on

yarn

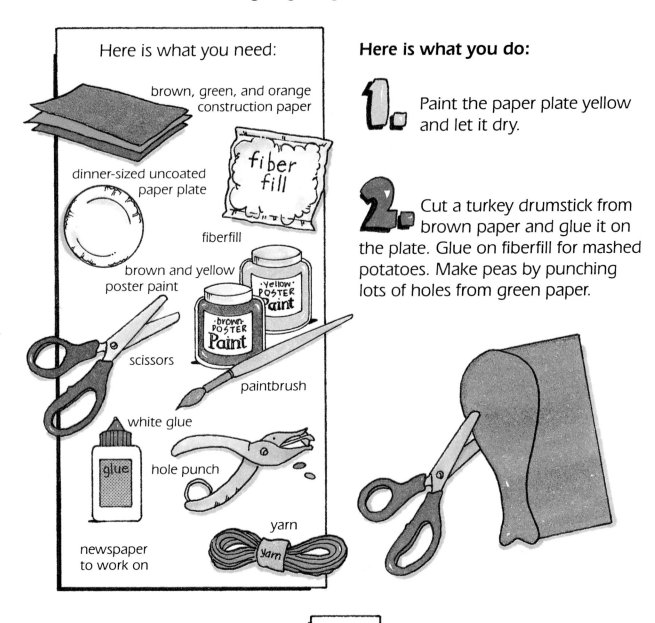

Here is what you do:

1. Paint the paper plate yellow and let it dry.

2. Cut a turkey drumstick from brown paper and glue it on the plate. Glue on fiberfill for mashed potatoes. Make peas by punching lots of holes from green paper.

Cut tiny carrot squares from orange paper. Mix the carrots and the peas and glue them on the plate. Drip some brown paint over the fiberfill to look like gravy.

3. Punch a hole in the top of the plate and run a loop of yarn through it for a hanger.

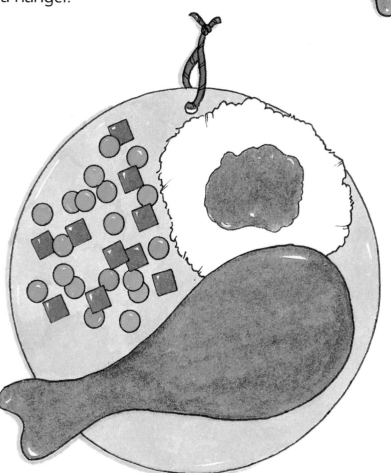

Your plate collage can also include foods that are a part of your family's Thanksgiving meal.

Play Food

You can pretend to serve your own Thanksgiving dinner as well as other favorite meals if you make a set of play food.

Here is what you need:

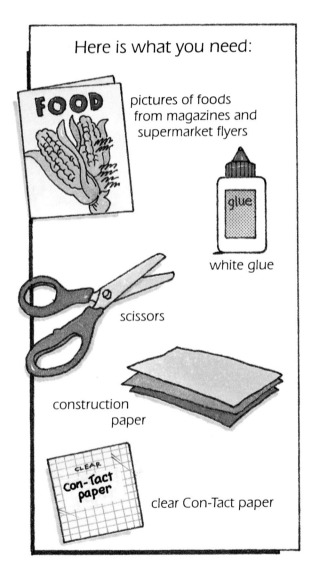

pictures of foods from magazines and supermarket flyers

white glue

scissors

construction paper

clear Con-Tact paper

Here is what you do:

1. Cut out pictures of lots of different kinds of foods. Choose pictures that are about the same size. Carefully cut out only the food, with no background, from each picture.

2. Glue each picture to construction paper. Let it dry and cut it out.

3. Cover both sides of each picture with a slightly larger piece of clear Con-Tact paper. Carefully cut out each food item again.

These sturdy goodies should last through hours of pretend dinners. Store them in a zip-to-close plastic bag when you are not using them.

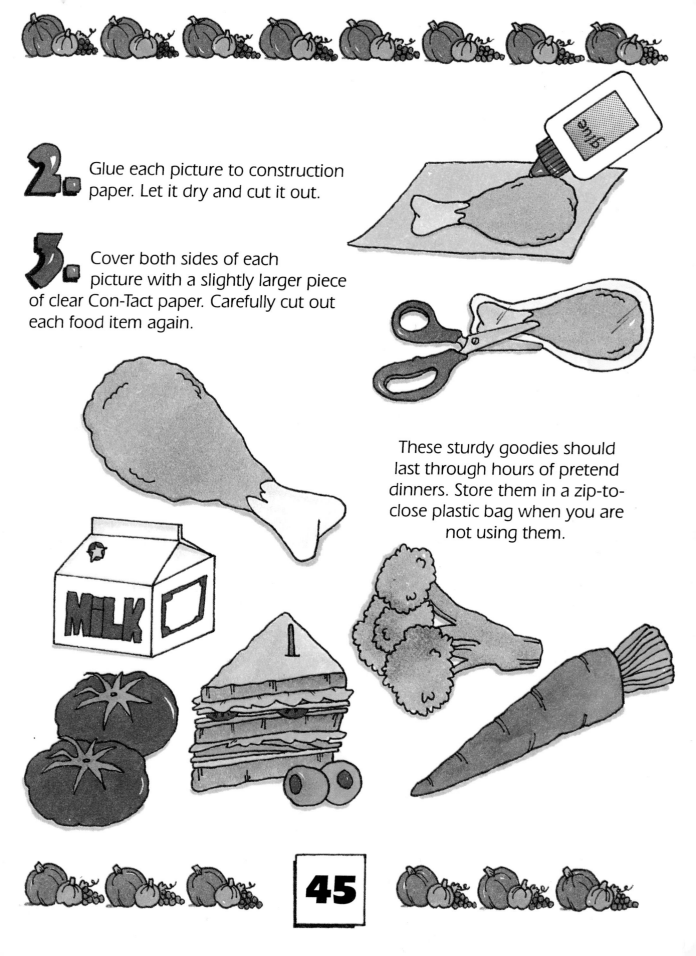

Family Photo Dolls

On Thanksgiving we are thankful for our families.

Here is what you need:

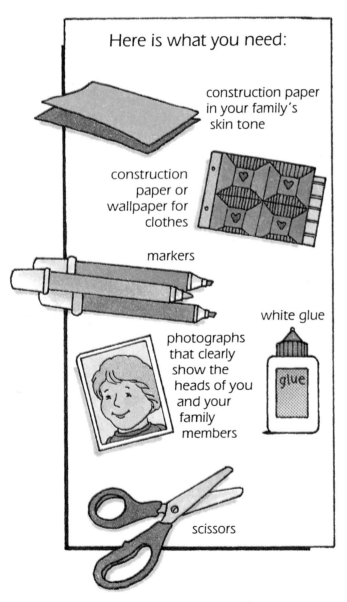

construction paper in your family's skin tone

construction paper or wallpaper for clothes

markers

white glue

glue

photographs that clearly show the heads of you and your family members

scissors

Here is what you do:

1. Draw the basic shape of each member of your family. You may want to make the dolls different sizes just as the people in your family are different sizes. Cut out your dolls.

2. In the photos of your family, find heads that will fit each doll. Carefully cut the heads out of the photos and glue them on the dolls.

3. Use markers to draw underclothes and shoes on your family dolls. Trace around each doll on wallpaper or construction paper to make clothing. You can glue the clothes on permanently or add tabs to the shoulders of the clothing and make lots of different outfits for each doll.

What will you and your family be thankful for this Thanksgiving?

About the Author and Illustrator

Twenty years as a teacher and director of nursery school programs have given Kathy Ross extensive experience in guiding young children through crafts projects. Her crafts have appeared in *Highlights* magazine, and she has also written numerous songs for children. She lives in Oneida, New York.

Sharon Lane Holm won awards for her work in advertising design before shifting her concentration to children's books. Her illustrations have since added zest to books for both the trade and education markets. She lives in New Fairfield, Connecticut.

Kathy Ross and Sharon Lane Holm have collaborated on these additional crafts books for kids: *Crafts for Kwanzaa, Crafts for Halloween, Crafts for Valentine's Day, Every Day Is Earth Day,* and *Crafts for Christmas.*